Do you see what I see?

The Art of Illusion

Prestel

Is it real or just a painting ...?

... that is the question! You really have to take a good look.

Trompe-l'œil is French and really means 'to trick the eye'. It is the name given to this type of painting.
As one story goes, a king was once given a picture like the one below. As he had never seen a painting like this before, he thought that everything was real and tried to pull out one of the painted pieces of paper! Back in the 17th century trompe-l'œil paintings were very popular, especially in Holland. Painters liked to try and show how good they were and such pictures drew a lot of attention to their work. But if you take a long look at the different things, don't you think that they start to look a bit strange—perhaps just because they have been painted in such detail?

SAMUEL VAN HOOGSTRATEN *Quodlibet*, 1666

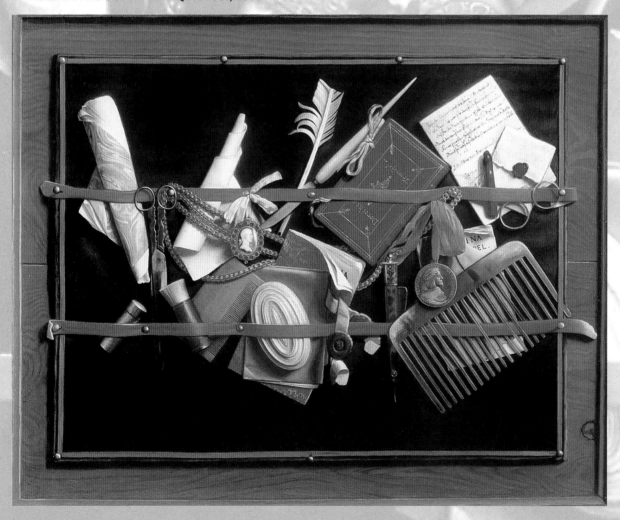

PABLO PICASSO *'Violin Jolie Eva'*, 1912

More than two hundred years later, many artists no longer wanted to paint objects just as we see them. Instead, each picture was to become a little world of its own. In this painting by Pablo Picasso, you can only tell that there is a violin by the strings and the sound-hole. On the other hand, the pieces of wood really do look real, just like in a trompe-l'œil painting. The artist is playing a clever game with bits and pieces from our everyday world placed next to shapes he has made up.

Is anyone there?

You certainly won't hear this young girl coming into the room! The Italian artist Paolo Veronese painted the picture of the girl and the whole doorway on one of the walls in the home of the Barbaro family in Italy, some 440 years ago. What fun he must have had making something look real which is not actually there and catching people out—or at least at first glance anyway!

There are all sorts of stories which were told about such paintings. Apparently a dog had a good sniff at a picture of another dog, while another went up to a portrait of its master wagging its tail, and a horse was frightened by a painting of another horse on a stable wall!

It wasn't long ago that the art of the Greeks and Romans became popular again and was used as a model. Even back in Ancient Rome, people painted their walls with views of the countryside to make a room look bigger and more interesting.

But that was nothing if you have a look at what was painted a couple of hundred years after Veronese in many of the grand palaces in Europe such as the one in Würzburg in Germany. The owner of the palace got the best painter of the day to work for him. His name was Giovanni Battista Tiepolo. Above the staircase and in the banqueting hall it looks as if the ceiling is open to the sky! The master painter from Italy played all sorts of tricks on the eye, mixing reality with illusion—or things that are not actually there. Have a look at the legs in the bottom, right-hand corner of the painting on the opposite page. Are they made of plaster or are they simply painted?

GIOVANNI BATTISTA TIEPOLO
The Genius of the German Empire, 1752–53

PAOLO VERONESE *Young Girl in the Door, c.* 1560

Is this a carving or a painting?

ANNE VALLAYER-COSTER *Satyrs and Children Playing with a Lioness*, painting of a carving (or relief as it is really called), 1776

Don't you think it looks as if the children playing here are made of plaster? You really have the feeling that you can touch them, don't you? But you'd be wrong—everything is perfectly flat! The children are simply painted on a piece of canvas.

How can a painter trick us so easily?

If you are very clever with your choice of colours and can paint very carefully, it is possible to paint pictures that look as if they are made of different materials. The use of the right amount of light and shadow can make something look rounded or give it depth, making it stand out from the background.

Up or down,

Ammonites

Sometimes shadows can create two opposite effects. These photos are of a fossil and its imprint. The shape that arches upwards is called convex and the one that goes down away from us is called concave. Now turn the book up side down and everything is switched around: the convex pictures look concave and the concave are convex.

MAURITS CORNELIS ESCHER *Concave and Convex*, 1955

raised
or sunken?

The Dutch painter Maurits Cornelis Escher thought up this amazing room full of concave and convex shapes. Are the columns in the middle sticking into or out of the page? Floors become ceilings and things inside are suddenly outside!

This is the parquet floor in the New Palace in Potsdam, near Berlin. The light and dark coloured pieces of wood make the floor look like a lot of cubes, and you can look at these cubes in different ways, too.

Tricks with perspective

RAPHAEL *The Betrothal of the Virgin*, 1504

Perspective is very important in art. It is a way of making things look as if they go away from us into a picture, giving it depth. You can work out the perspective by taking a close look at things or by using mathematics.

In the 15th century, the Italians found out the rules of perspective. This painting by Raphael shows how these rules can be used. In the painting, lines that are actually parallel to each other are shown running together towards an unseen point in the distance.
The further the people and objects are away from the artist, the smaller they become. Our eyes deal with the way we see things in a similar way and, as a result, objects in the distance look small. Our brain works automatically so that things are not out of focus, even if we don't notice this at all.

Raphael painted the countryside in the background of the painting in a slightly blurred, bluish colour. This blends very well with the sky. Perspective pictures like this draw our eye far into the distance.

A famous German artist, Albrecht Dürer, made a tool to help draw things in perspective. A piece of string has been fixed to a point from which an object, in this case a musical instrument, is to be drawn. The string is then moved around the instrument—a lute—and a hole is pricked into the piece of paper using a pin to mark each position. By joining up the pinpricks a picture of the lute drawn correctly in perspective appears.

ALBRECHT DÜRER *Instructions in Perspectives: Drawing a Lute*, 1525

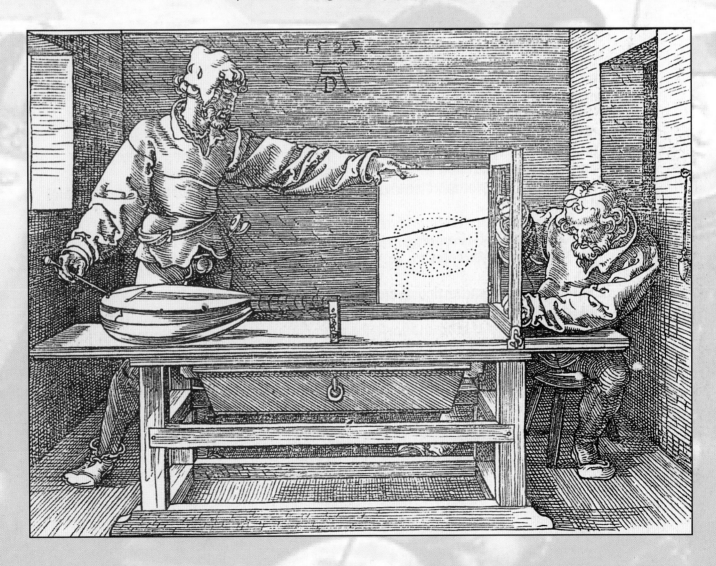

Giants and dwarfs

It may be difficult to
believe, but these three
figures are the same size!
The one on the right
looks like a giant and
the one on the left like
a dwarf. This is because
of the lines that get closer
and closer to each other.
They make it look as if
the room goes back a long
way. The man on the left
seems to be very close
to us and the man on the
right the furthest away
—even though he is
no smaller than the
others. From what we
see every day, we know
that somebody further
away has to be very tall
to look bigger than
a figure closer to us.

Is this the 'giant' Gulliver on his travels to the land of the little people in Lilliput? Or have the pictures of the two people been stuck onto another photograph? It is neither of these, in fact. We are looking into an unusually shaped room which makes a normal person look either like a dwarf or a giant! The room is not square—the back wall slopes backwards from the right to the left and the floor in the back left-hand corner is much lower than on the right. The man in the left-hand picture is actually much further back and lower down than the boy. (They have changed places in the other photo). If you look into the room with one eye through a little hole at just the right place in the wall, as in the photos, you cannot tell that the back wall slopes away from us or that the floor goes down. Instead, it looks as if there is a dwarf next to a huge chair and a giant in the other corner of a square room! If you could look into the room with both eyes you would see straight away that this is a trick—or an optical illusion, as it is called— and you would see how far back the room really goes.

Jan Dibbets is from Holland and, like many artists working today, he is interested in the way we see things. In the photo on the left, the further the posts are from the viewer, the bigger they are. The perspective in this photo looks as if it is wrong, doesn't it? We would normally expect to find a row of posts of the same size which would then look smaller and smaller the further back they go. That is why the artist called this piece *Perspective correction*.

JAN DIBBETS *Perspective correction – 5 poles*, 1967

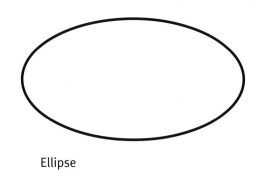

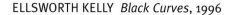
Ellipse

Are they the same or are they different?

The geometrical shape above is called
an ellipse. The same shape appears
again in the drawing next to it where
it is a round hoop, which is shown
from the side.

And what is this? Is it a rectangle seen
from an unusual perspective?
The American artist Ellsworth Kelly
has not used a rectangular canvas
but one with a sloping top and bottom
and curved sides. He calls this a
'shaped canvas'. As we would expect
a regular shape with right angles,
we automatically think that this is a
rectangle from a strange perspective.

ELLSWORTH KELLY *Black Curves*, 1996

Do you think that anyone would ever say that the doors below get bigger from left to right? No, of course they wouldn't! Everybody knows what a door looks like, and all these doors are the same. But in each picture the opening gets smaller and smaller. The different shape of each door is due to the perspective.

GERHARD RICHTER *Five Doors*, 1967

But what is on the other side of the doors? The artist hasn't painted an imaginary room. Instead there is nothing there at all!

Coded messages

What do you think that mark is on the floor in the painting on the opposite page? Perhaps the artist didn't finish the picture, or do you think someone may have damaged it?

The answer to the question is quite simple. Look at the painting straight on and, tipping the page up as if turning it, take a closer look at the mark from the right. Your nose should almost be touching the right-hand edge of the book.

The mark now turns into a skull! It is a symbol for the death of the man on the left who was no longer alive when Hans Holbein painted the two ambassadors.

Sometimes artists hid symbols in their paintings and made up a type of secret language which could only be understood by those who knew about such things.

But other times artists just liked painting from odd perspectives as a way of letting people know how good they were, as in the example here on the left, which is a portrait of the boy king Edward VI.

WILLIAM SCROTS *Portrait of King Edward VI*, 1546

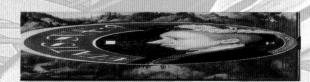

HANS HOLBEIN THE YOUNGER *The Ambassadors*, 1533

That can't be true—or can it?

Drawing in perspective can be difficult. First of all you have to train your eye to see things as they are and then learn how to draw or paint them. The English artist William Hogarth must have had fun making this print (*right*) in which he has added a number of mistakes which artists often made. How can the woman in the window possibly light the pipe smoked by the man behind the house on the hill? How can the man with the fishing rod in the front of the picture actually get the fish out of the water? Looking at the size of the sheep on the left makes you think of the men on page 10 again, doesn't it? There are all sorts of things here that are just not possible!

WILLIAM HOGARTH *False Perspective*, 1753

The graphic artist Maurits Cornelis Escher came up with some amazing ways to show depth and space on a flat surface. He drew three-dimensional scenes which are only possible on paper or canvas!

What a strange looking building this is on the right! The man sitting on the bench has an impossibly shaped cube in his hands, which seems like a model for the impossibly shaped building! The drawing lying on the ground gives us a clue as to why the building looks the way it does.

In the first drawing of the cube at the bottom of the page, either the corners 1 and 4 are closest to us and 2 and 3 further away or the other way around— like the parquet floor on page 7. However you can also try and imagine corners 2 and 4 closest to us and 1 and 3 in the background or vice-versa. This is made clearer in the second drawing where the lines are thicker. But you would never be able to make such a cube!

The top and bottom levels of this building are perfectly normal on their own, but the way they have been combined makes it physically impossible, just like the cube.

MAURITS CORNELIS ESCHER *Belvedere*, 1958

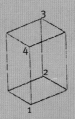  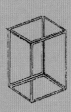

How many birds are there?

Watch out when counting! There are more than you would think at first glance.

Blue-coloured birds are flying around in the sunlight. Their dark outlines contrast with the bright sky.
But if you look at the gaps between them, you will find a lot of white-coloured birds against a deep-blue night sky, with a crescent-shaped moon and several stars.

Normally figures stand out clearly from what is behind them, especially when they are smaller than the background and have a clear shape. In this picture, however, all the white and blue-coloured areas are in the shape of birds and all are the same size.

MAURITS CORNELIS ESCHER *Sun and Moon, 1948*

Here is another bird.
Bright and clear, it is flying
over the waves against
the cloudy evening sky.
But its feathers look so
strange, don't they? Then
the bird seems to disappear
as the clouds part and we
see little white clouds and
a brilliant blue sky!
The Belgian painter René
Magritte wanted to show
that, behind everything
you see, there is always
something else.

RENE MAGRITTE *The Big Family*, 1936

Hidden pictures

There are many surprises hidden in this landscape by Salvador Dalí. The artist painted more than just a picture of the beach at Cape Creus in Spain where he often stayed, showing the sea and the cliffs, a couple of boats and a woman, seen from behind, mending the sail. Nothing in this picture is quite as it appears at first sight. Can you see how the cliffs, the water and the seated woman turn into a bowl of fruit which, in turn, becomes a man's face? The bow of the boat in the foreground can also be seen as a traditional musical instrument— a mandolin. And where are the greyhound, the 'philosopher' and the horse? Dalí himself gave the answers to these questions by making a number of drawings which show the many different ways of looking at this painting.

Like René Magritte, Salvador Dalí was a Surrealist painter. These artists were interested in things that went 'beyond reality'; in other words for connections between things which we may not see straight away.

Dalí gave this painting the title *The Endless Enigma*. Even when you can find all the different objects and figures hidden in the painting, it is still difficult to work out exactly what is what.

The children's book illustrator Julian Jusim has hidden a squirrel and a fox is this picture. Can you find them?

JULIAN JUSIM, illustration in *When Little Rabbits go to Bed*, 2000

SALVADOR DALÍ *The Endless Enigma*, 1938

SALVADOR DALÍ, drawings for *The Endless Enigma*

 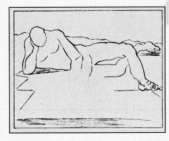  

Is red red and green green?

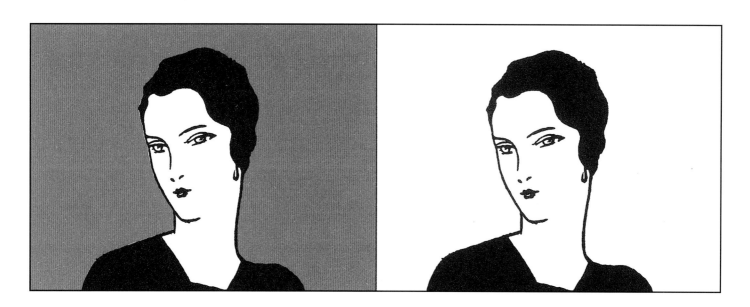

Or are things sometimes different from the way they first appear? Take a look at the picture above on the left. Stare at it for about twenty seconds in good light, without moving your eyes, and then look straight at the picture on the right.

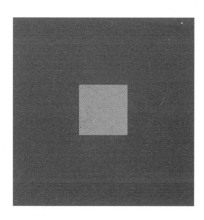

The brightness of the red makes our eyes tired. To balance this, we see the colour green. Our eyes do this automatically without actually seeing anything green. Is it magic? How do such things work? It's quite simple really. Green is the opposite colour to red. Every colour has an opposite. The brighter the colour and the longer you look at it, the more intensively the opposite colour appears. Brilliant colours can even cause the opposite colour to be seen at the same time. The grey colour in the two little squares is perfectly plain—no other colours have been added. Yet if you look closely you will see that the grey square against the red background has a greenish shimmer to it, while the grey square against the green background looks reddish. The same is true for the picture above on the right. As the opposite colour appears at the same time, the woman's face blushes slightly.

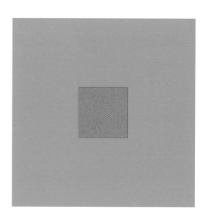

Josef Albers painted a series of pictures which show squares in different colour combinations.
He was looking closely at the different effects of colours when put next to each other.
Look at the light-green square and, after a little while, a light-violet coloured shimmer will appear
around this square, being the opposite colour to light green.

JOSEF ALBERS *Homage to the Square: Renewed Hope*, 1962

Cheerful red and shy blue

Some colours love to be noticed and others keep themselves in the background. All warm and bright colours, especially yellow, orange and red, jump out at us and are always in the foreground. Cold and softer colours draw our eyes back into the depths of a picture. That is perhaps why Samuel van Hoogstraten painted the leather straps across the painting on page 4 in red. They come right into the foreground and hold the objects in place.

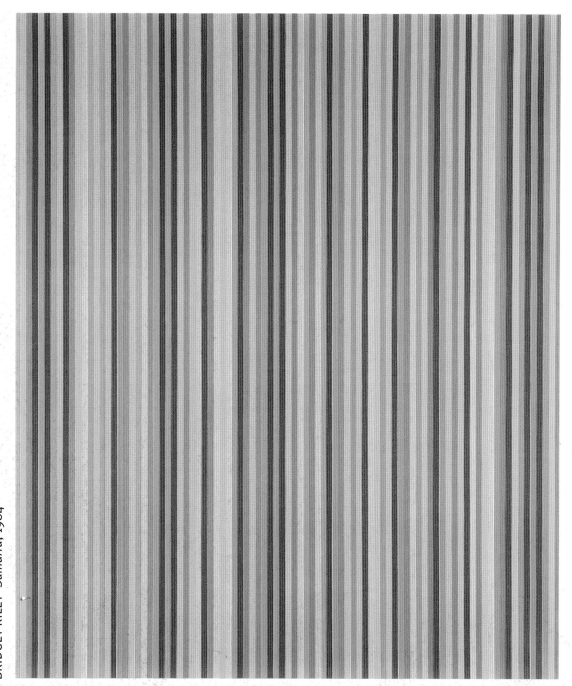

BRIDGET RILEY *Samarra*, 1984

The feeling you get of space or depth depends on which colours are next to each other. In this painting by the English artist Bridget Riley, the red and yellow stripes seem to be closest to us. The bluish stripes look the furthest away. The light-pink stripes only stand out if there are two relatively strong colours on either side. The light blue comes up quite strongly in a few places. Green can stay in the background but it can just as easily push its way into the foreground, too.

BRIDGET RILEY *Crest,* 1964

Here, the artist is playing with the contrast between black and white. But take a longer look at the waves and you will notice that light, pastel shades of colour will appear.

Moving pictures

You don't have to go to the cinema if you want to see pictures in motion! Not everything that moves has to be in a film! These paintings seem to be in motion too, although not a single line or colour actually moves!

The Swiss artist Richard Paul Lohse created this picture based on the spectrum—red, violet, indigo, blue, green, yellow, orange and back to red again. Wherever similar, light colours appear next to each other, the picture begins to shimmer.

RICHARD PAUL LOHSE Thirty vertical and systematically arranged colour strips with red diagonals, 1943–70

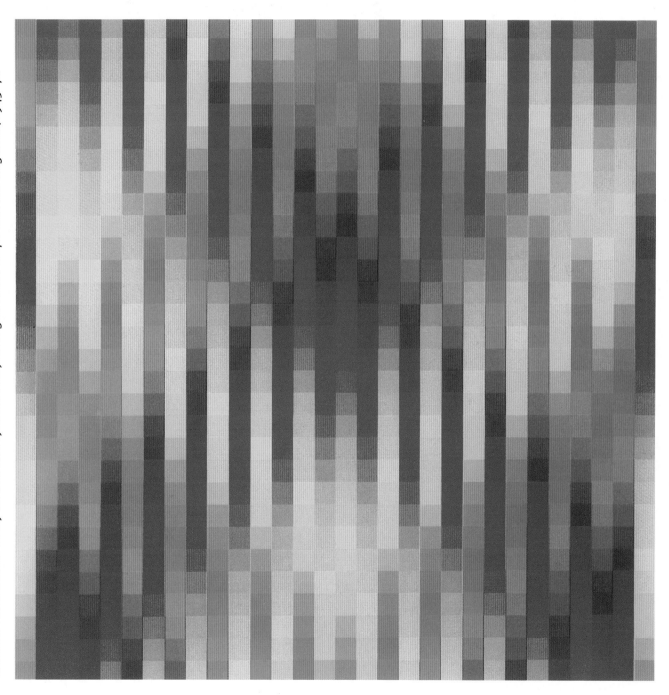

26

VICTOR VASARELY *Zint +*, 1952/60

The 'inner eye' sees white as the opposite to black, and black as the opposite to white. Since some of the lines run very close to each other, we keep seeing the opposite colours which make the picture seem as if it is moving.

There are also many lines in the painting which change direction and this too makes the picture 'move'. The Hungarian artist Victor Vasarely, like Bridget Riley, is very interested in the way we see things and so-called optical effects.

This type of art has been given the name Op-Art, which is short for optical art.

The illustrations in this book

Front cover:
RENÉ MAGRITTE, *The Human Condition*, 1935
Oil on canvas, 100 × 73 cm
Private Collection, Monte Carlo

MAURITS CORNELIS ESCHER
Drawing Hands, 1948
Lithography, 28.5 × 34 cm

Picture puzzle: Portraits / Vase

Picture puzzle: Witch / Young Woman

Pages 2/3:
SAMUEL VAN HOOGSTRATEN, *Quodlibet*, 1666
Oil on canvas, 63 × 79 cm
Staatliche Kunsthalle, Karlsruhe

PABLO PICASSO, *Violin 'Jolie Eva'*, 1912
Oil on canvas, 60 × 81 cm
Staatsgalerie, Stuttgart

Pages 4/5:
PAOLO VERONESE
Young Girl in the Door, c. 1560
Fresco
Villa Barbaro, Maser

GIOVANNI BATTISTA TIEPOLO
The Genius of the German Empire, 1752–53
Ceiling fresco, 9 x 18 m
The Residence, Würzburg

Pages 6/7:
ANNE VALLAYER-COSTER, *Satyrs and Children Playing with a Lioness*, 1776
Painted imitation of a bas-relief, oil on canvas, 30 × 40 cm
Private Collection

MAURITS CORNELIS ESCHER
Concave and Convex, 1955
Lithography, 27.5 × 33.5 cm

Parquet floor in Friedrich II's study, 1765
Wood parquet, New Palais, Potsdam

Pages 8/9:
RAPHAEL, *The Betrothal of the Virgin*
(*La sposalizio della Vergine*), 1504
Oil on wood, 170 × 118 cm
Pinacoteca di Brera, Milan

ALBRECHT DÜRER, *Instructions in Perspectives: Drawing a Lute*, 1525
From: *Instructions in Taking Measurements*
Book woodcut, 13.2 × 18.2 cm (size of image)

Pages 10/11:
JAN DIBBETS
Perspective Correction – 5 Poles, 1967
Black-and-white photograph on pencil on photographic canvas, 50 × 65 cm
Private Collection

Pages 12/13:
ELLSWORTH KELLY, *Black Curves*, 1996
Oil on canvas, 365.5 × 108 cm
Private Collection

GERHARD RICHTER, *Five Doors*, 1967
Oil on canvas, 5 parts, 205 × 100 cm each
Museum Ludwig, Cologne

Pages 14/15:
WILLIAM SCROTS, *King Edward VI*, 1546
Oil on panel, 42.5 × 160 cm
The National Portrait Gallery, London

HANS HOLBEIN THE YOUNGER
The Ambassadors, 1533
Oil on oak wood, 207 × 209.5 cm
The National Gallery, London

Pages 16/17:
WILLIAM HOGARTH, *False Perspective*, 1753
Etching

MAURITS CORNELIS ESCHER, *Belvedere*, 1958
Lithography, 46 × 29.5 cm

Pages 18/19:
MAURITS CORNELIS ESCHER, *Sun and Moon*, 1948
Woodcut, printed with two printing blocks, 39.1 × 67.7 cm

RENÉ MAGRITTE, *The Big Family*, 1936
Oil on canvas, 100 × 81 cm
Private Collection

Pages 20/21:
JULIAN JUSIM, illustration from: *When Little Rabbits Go to Sleep*, Beltz & Gelberg, Weiheim/Basel, 2000

SALVADOR DALÍ, *The Endless Enigma*, 1938
Oil on canvas, 114.5 × 146.5 cm
Private Collection

SALVADOR DALÍ, drawings for *The Endless Enigma*. Facsimile from the catalogue accompanying the Dalí exhibition at the Julien Levy Gallery in New York (March/April 1939)

Pages 22/23:
JOSEF ALBERS, *Homage to the Square: Renewed Hope*, 1962
Oil on hard board, 121.5 × 121.5 cm
Westfälisches Landesmuseum für Kunst und Kulturgeschichte, Münster

Pages 24/25:
BRIDGET RILEY, *Samarra*, 1984
Oil on canvas, 203.5 × 173 cm
Courtesy Karsten Schubert, London

BRIDGET RILEY, *Crest*, 1964
Emulsion paint on cardboard, 166.5 × 166.5 cm
The British Council, London

Pages 26/27:
RICHARD PAUL LOHSE, *Thirty vertical systematically arranged colour strips with red diagonals*, 1943–70
Oil on canvas, 165 × 165 cm
Richard Paul Lohse Foundation, Zurich

VICTOR VASARELY, *Zint +*, 1952/60
Tempera on cardboard, 40 × 36.5 cm
Collection Karin and Berthold Müller

Back cover:
WILLIAM HOGARTH
False Perspective, see page 16